Dedicated to my beautiful family- Francis, Arunothai, Naroote, Gift, Aunchisa, Shane, Mikaela & Ariya. I love you all.

ISBN 978-616-455-561-7

Book Design by Kanokpat Jiraphan
Editing by Tan Lay Leng
Published by Aarksara

Distributed by
AMARIN BOOK CENTER CO.,LTD
108 Moo2 Bang Kruai – Jongthanom Road,
Maha Sawat, Bang Kruai, Nonthaburi 11130
Tel. 02-423-9999
Fax. 0-2449-9222, 0-2449-9500-6
Homepage : http://www.naiin.com

About Aarksara

ABOUT AARKSARA:
Born in Singapore and raised and educated in Australia and Canada, Aarksara has a dream to touch her nation and the nations of this world with her songs and vocal training courses that transcend cultural differences and barriers.

Aarksara has been featured on various radio stations and magazine publications. She graduated with a Bachelor of Commerce degree from The University of Western Australia as well as a Specialist Certificate in General Music Studies from Berklee College of Music, Boston. She is currently undertaking New York Singing Teachers' Association's Distinguished Voice Professional Certification Program.

Aarksara travels the world frequently to train and equip vocalists with fresh and inspiring ways to increase and improve their vocal skills. With internationally acclaimed music producers including Grammy-nominated and Dove Award winning producer Rusty Varenkamp and also Colin Mills from Closet Audio Productions, she has released her debut album 'Made It Through'. She is regularly commissioned to co-write for other artists and organisations on various projects.

Endorsements:

Aarksara has created the perfect guide of necessary and practical tools for all singers, beginners to advanced, to enhance their vocal skills

- Charlin Neal, Vocal Director of Israel & New Breed

Aarksara reveals the secrets of a professional vocalist. She breaks it down so that anyone can understand, practice and make it work

- Wern Ruangkit, Music Producer, Composer

A fun guideline to improving your singing skills. It's like Aarksara's in front of you telling you to do silly things but they really do work!

- Rose Sirintip, Grammy Artist

Aarksara's gifts don't just end with her singing...She also stands out as a wonderfully gifted educator. This guide is a must-have for vocal enthusiasts (and professionals) willing to brush up on their skills!

- Joe Zamudio, The Voice Thailand

Aarksara is as legit as it gets! She's the real deal!

- Jerry Chua, Grammy Nominated Mixing & Mastering Engineer

Endorsements:

An amazing book that will add value to your worship ministry singers. Aarksara's approach is direct and practical. Any student will find that this book will enrich and complement their vocal training.

- Pastor Andrew Yeo, Worship Pastor,
Cornerstone Community Church Singapore

Aarksara is a talented and gifted teacher/singer/songwriter. She is passionate about equipping and teaching people to be the best they can be.

- Michelle Rossi, Planetshakers Vocalist

I had the awesome privilege of meeting Aarksara at the very first vocal summit in Bangkok and Singapore, which was organized through U Wonder. It was quickly evident that this young lady was a force to reckon with.
I was blessed to share the stage teaching with her. Her passion for empowering others to sing better is undeniable. Her desire to bring the best of the world to Asian culture is what drives her. I believe that through this book, you will not only see her heart for people but more than anything her skill in the form of well crafted, practical ways to help you sing better by understanding your voice and how to use it well.

- Lois DuPlessis, International Vocalist & Actor

CHAPTER ONE

Vocal Foundations

Breathing:

The number one question I ask all my clients and students in their introductory lessons is "As singers, where do we breathe from?" The question is usually received with a bit of confusion. Some would answer that we breathe in through our nose. Technically, that is not an incorrect answer. I would further challenge them to breathe through their nose and sing a phrase from one of their favourite songs. They usually could not make it past the second line! This is why for a singer, having breath support by our diaphragm is very useful. Imagine that before you sing, you're an empty tank and you need to 'fill that tank' by taking a big breath in with the help of your diaphragm. Our diaphragm supports our vocal cords by automatically expanding.

Let's start with one exercise that can further demonstrate this concept. If you're sitting down or standing up whilst doing this exercise, please relax your shoulders. Posture is very important for singers. Place one hand on your abdominal muscles just below your belly button. Breathe in. Do you feel your rib cage expanding? As you breathe in, your belly should be pushing against your hand. As you breathe out, your belly should be contracting back into position. Let me say it this way : Breathe in- your tummy should look somewhat pregnant. Breathe out- your tummy should contract back into your 'six-pack' position (or so we wish!). Do this exercise 5 times. Breathe in, breathe out - YOU GOT IT! Well done!

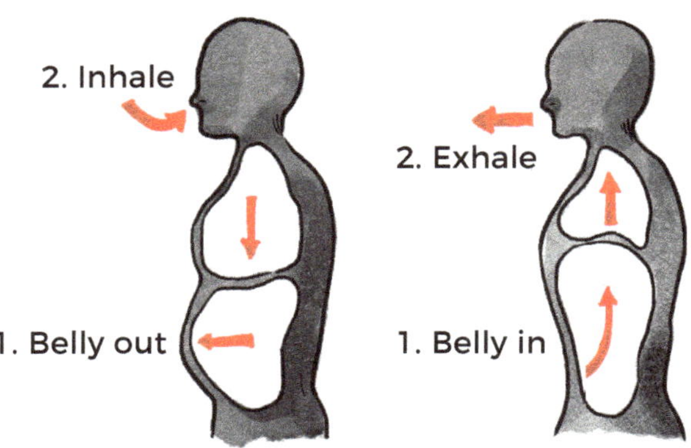

Now, lie on the floor. Lie completely flat on the floor. Grab a heavy book and place it on your tummy just underneath your rib cage. Take a big breath in so that the book rises. Hold this for 5 seconds, then release. Repeat 3 times.

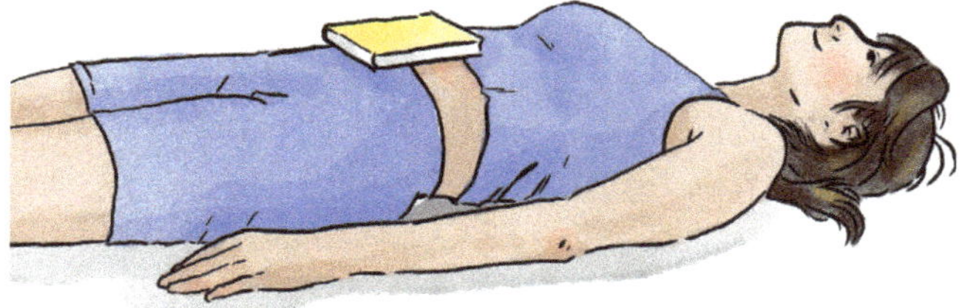

Two Important Factors in Voice:

1. Air Function/Airflow
2. Vocal Placement

Air Function or Airflow is how fast or slow air is passing through our mouth. If we don't have enough air coming through, the notes we sing tend to fall flat. Flat notes are notes that are sung and pitched below the intended note. If we have too much air coming through, the notes we sing tend to sound sharp. Sharp notes are notes that are sung and pitched above the intended note. **Vocal Placement** requires singers to properly position

their larynx so that the best possible sound is produced with ease.
If the voice is not properly placed or the airflow is compensated, singers will resort to squeezing and tightening their neck muscles. Resorting to these measures only distorts the sound and creates more problems

Let's move on to our next exercise. Wherever you are right now, please yawn for me. C'mon you can yawn bigger than that! But please, don't fall asleep on me. We are only at Chapter 1 of this book. Do you feel the 'openness' at the back of your throat? It's a relaxing sensation, yes? Yawn for me one more time. I want you to always have this 'yawning' sensation every time you sing. There should be no tension or pain. The larynx and tongue are relaxed.

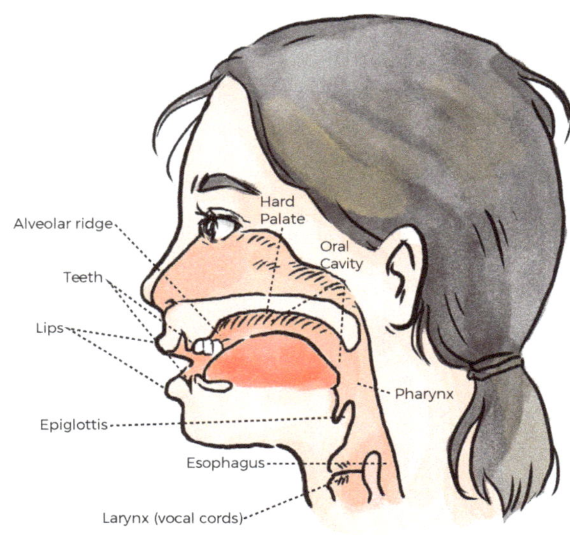

Diction:

How many times do you find yourself in a conversation and you completely misunderstand what the person is trying to say due to his or her poor pronunciation? As singers, we do not want that to happen when we sing! We want to make sure we communicate clearly the message or story of the song enunciating our words through our voice. We refer to this as diction. Here are some tongue twisters to improve your diction. Start slow, then gradually speak faster:

1. Peter Piper :
Peter Piper picked a peck of pickled peppers. Did Peter Piper pick a peck of pickled peppers? If Peter Piper picked a peck of pickled peppers, where's the peck of pickled peppers Peter Piper picked?

2. Woodchuck :
How much wood would a woodchuck chuck if a woodchuck could chuck wood? He would chuck, he would, as much as he could, and chuck as much wood as a woodchuck would if a woodchuck could chuck wood.

3. Ice Cream :
I scream, you scream, we all scream for ice cream!

4. Fuzzy Wuzzy :
Fuzzy Wuzzy was a bear. Fuzzy Wuzzy had no hair. Fuzzy Wuzzy wasn't very fuzzy, was he?

5. Betty Botter :

Betty Botter had some butter,"But", she said, "this butter's better. If I bake this bitter butter, it would make my batter bitter. But a bit of better butter- that would make my batter better." So she bought a bit of butter, better than her bitter butter and she baked it in her batter, and the batter was not bitter. So 'twas better Betty Botter bought a bit of better butter.

6. She Sells Sea Shells :

She sells sea shells by the sea shore. The shells she sells are surely seashells. So if she sells shells on the seashore, I'm sure she sells seashore shells.

7. I Thought :

I thought a thought. But the thought I thought wasn't the thought I thought I thought.

Three Widely Used Voices in Singing

There are three widely used voices singers can utilize.
I like to say they are three different approaches singers can put in their singers' toolbox. The first one is **chest voice.** This voice resonates predominantly in the chest. It creates a rich, deep and full timbre. The second one is **head voice.** This voice resonates predominantly in the head. It usually produces a softer and airier sound. The third voice is the **mixed voice.** This is a combination of head and chest voice. Please note that different singers 'break' at different passages, hence they would tap into their chest, head and mixed voices at different notes.

Sing through this chromatic scale to 'OH' and note where you use your **chest voice, head voice and mixed voice.**

'Oh' Exercise

CHAPTER TWO

Mastering Performance Technique

It is very important as singers to not only convey the message of the song confidently through our voice, but also through our stage presence. There's a difference between being arrogant and exuding a quiet yet bold confidence. Looking like a star whilst performing is really a matter of confidence and boldness. You may get nervous singing in front of your family but do you know that even artists who sing in front of audience of thousands still get cold feet? It's OK! Just practice your performance and use those nerves to your advantage. Enjoy the moment, enjoy performing and blessing the world with your God-given gifts!

Stand in front of a mirror and sing your favourite song. Blast out the track on your phone or other audio devices. Use any object as your 'microphone'. How did you go? Did you look stiff like a tree or were you relaxed and enjoying yourself?

Mastering Performance technique requires us to practice working the microphone, the stand, the stage, your fellow band members, and most importantly your own body so that you will gain a confidence that will enable you to pull off the performance with great joy and excellence!

If you want to walk over to the right side of the stage, then move there with a purpose. Don't waddle over meekly, or say 'excuse me, whilst I move to the right'. Move with confidence and clarity. If you want to use your hands or facial expressions, go ahead! Just make sure that you do it with purpose and authenticity. You are not a puppet! Relax! I tell my clients and students, that as singers, we must be able to express not only through voice but also through our body language and facial expressions. Tell the story using everything you've been given: your heart, body and soul!

Correct Microphone Technique

Coping With Stage Fright- Mastering Performance Checklist:

- BREATHE!
- Recognise that you may feel a bit nervous but tell yourself it's OK. You've worked hard on this performance and you're going to do great!
- Use the emotions and passion you feel for the performance and express it! Don't suppress it! GO FOR IT!
- Tell yourself: everyone here is FOR you not against you! Enjoy yourself.

This time, stand in front of a mirror again and sing your favourite song. Blast out the track on your phone or other audio devices. Use any object as your 'microphone'. Do a little bit of choreography. Move here and there, with purpose. Use your hands, close your eyes. EXPRESS YOURSELF! Be YOU!

CHAPTER THREE

Vocal Dynamics

Dynamics are tools that bring your voice or song to LIFE! They help convey emotions and prevent performances and voices from sounding static or boring. Imagine watching a movie and the same scene is played over and over again for the whole duration of the movie, you would get very bored! You may even walk out of the cinema! It's the same with singers. If they are not using vocal dynamics, it can quickly turn into a very boring and mediocre performance. In the previous chapter, you read that when you want to tell a story, you must take the listener on a journey with you When singers use vocal dynamics effectively, it can result in the listener feeling moved or convicted of a certain emotion or feeling.

Vocal Dynamic Tools

Crescendo and Decrescendo (Diminuendo):

Crescendo is a gradual increase in loudness in a piece of music. **Decrescendo** is a gradual decrease in loudness in a piece of music. Singers can increase their volume in their vocals when they reach the most emotional part of the song (usually that's the chorus). Singers can decrease volume in their vocals if they want to create a contrast between the emotional high part of the song, pulling back to create a 'stillness' effect.

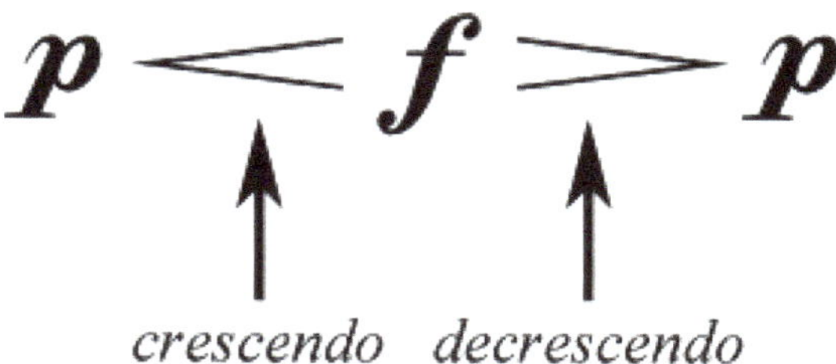

Vocal Dynamic Exercise

SOFT — LOUD — SOFT

a) MAH ________________________________

b) MEE ________________________________

c) MOH ________________________________

Baa Baa Black Sheep Exercise

pp *Pianissimo, Very Soft*

p *Piano, Soft*

mp *Mezzo-Piano, Half Soft*

mf *Mezzo-Forte, Half Loud*

f *Forte, Loud*

ff *Fortissimo, Very Loud*

Diction/Articulation:

As mentioned in our earlier chapters, diction/articulation is a crucial part in a Singer's Toolbox. Mumbling through a song will easily disengage the singer. We need to ensure we are pronouncing our words clearly and with characterisation.

Adding Vocal Rests

Adding vocal rests creates an extra dimension to the song. By including these vocal rests, it allows the listener to pause and ponder on what they have heard so far. Remember, we want to bring the audience on an emotional journey!

CHAPTER FOUR

Vocal Tones & Timbres

I LOVE colours! Friends and family who come over to my home will know I love pastel colours. From my kitchen appliances to my bed sheets and cushions, I love mixing and matching beautiful colours to add more life to my home. Many who have walked through my front doors would say, "This is definitely Aarksara's house!" (I'm taking this as a compliment!) It's the same with singers, the moment someone hears your voice, their reaction should be "Ah..this is so and so's voice." Why? Because each of our voices has distinct and unique qualities and characteristics. We use the terms Tones & Timbres to describe the unique qualities and characteristics in voices. Tones and Timbres are interchangeable. Timbre is the emotional description of your voice. Some words to describe timbres are: clear, bright, rich, focused, unfocused, mellow, harsh, heavy, warm, flat, light etc. Tones and Timbres are not characterized by frequency (pitch), duration (rhythm), or amplitude (volume). We can use colour associations to help us describe a singer's Voice Tone & Timbre.

Here are a list of colours...can you describe
a "vocal timbre" next to each colour?

CHAPTER FIVE

Vocal Health Development & Enhancement

This is one of my favourite Vocal topics! I love everything to do with health and nutrition. Since our voice is an instrument of flesh and blood, diet is more important for singers than it is for other types of musicians.

Singers need to pay special attention to what we put in our bodies, especially on the days before a performance. A bad diet could be the cause of the production of too much phlegm (mucous) or the drying out of your vocal cords.

As singers, we need to take care of our vocal health, as we do not want to experience any vocal abuse or vocal fatigue. Vocal Abuse occurs after extensive singing or speaking. The inside of the larynx becomes sore resulting in the voice becoming excessively breathy. Vocal Fatigue results in singers being unable to vocalize for a long period of time. Some may experience nodules, which are tiny callous-like bumps on vocal cords or polyps, which are lesions that are formed after a blood vessel is broken, similar to a blister.

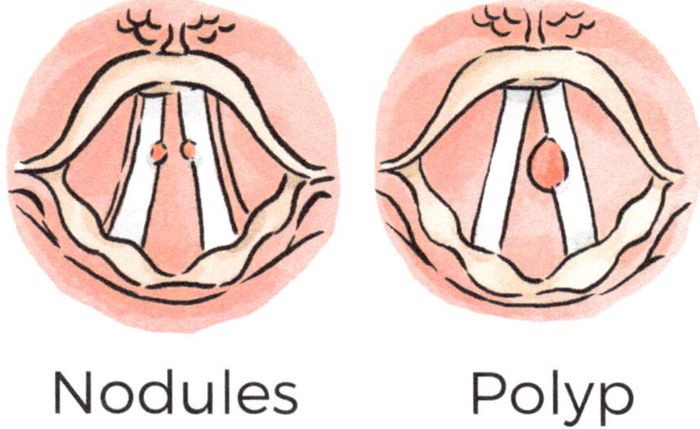

Nodules Polyp

Hence, it is very important to make sure we give some extra love to our vocal health! Here is a Singer's Nutrition table where you can fill in the blank spaces with food and drinks that affect your voice.

Singer's Nutrition

Singer Friendly Foods:	Singer Deadly Foods:
WATER!!	Milk products
Herbal teas	MSG
Non-citrus fruits	Excessive alcohol
Pasta	Refined sugars
Eggs	Smoking
Vegetables	Caffeine
Lean meats	Artificial sweeteners
	Junk food
	Spicy Foods

* Please note that each of us has a unique body chemistry. Some are completely unaffected by anything they eat/drink, whilst others can have severe reactions.

- Drink lots of room-temperature water
- Eat high water content fruit for hydration and energy
- Eat high water content vegetables for hydration and minerals
- Don't drink coffee or caffeinated drinks within two to three hours prior to singing
- Don't drink iced drinks within two to three hours prior to singing

Not only is it important to watch what we eat and drink before a performance, we must also make sure we warm up and warm down our vocal cords properly. For those who exercise, you know that if you don't stretch before you work out, you are at a high risk of injuring yourself or feeling incredibly sore the following day. It's the same for singing, if we don't warm up and stretch our vocal cords appropriately, we could send them into a shock and possibly harm or damage them temporarily or permanently. We have been given a beautiful set of vocal cords, so let's make sure we take care of them!

Vocal Warm Ups :

1. Humming:

Practice humming the C Major scale. Go up and down the scale. Relax, just hum! Humming is a fantastic vocal warm up to do before a performance, especially if you're a bit tight for time!

Humming Exercise

2. Sirens:

This is a great exercise to open up your throat and relax your larynx. I want you to shape your mouth with the vowel 'Ooo'. Start low in your chest voice and gradually build up higher into your head voice. Make sure you don't break, make it as smooth as possible! Imagine you're going up a vocal rollercoaster. Ready. 1 2 3.....'Oooooooooo'.

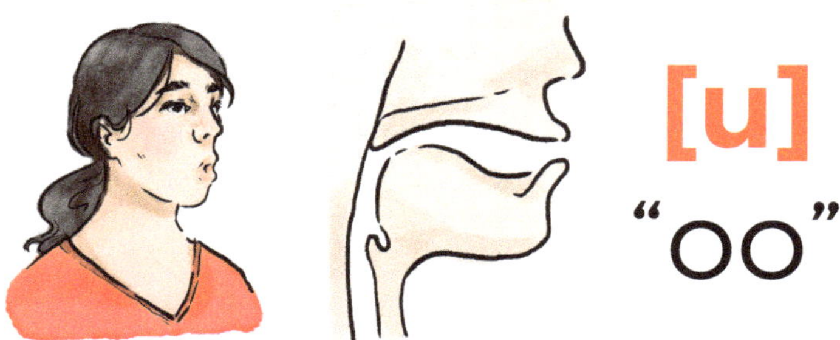

3. Lip Rolls:

Lip Rolls are one of my favourite vocal warm ups! Gently place your two index fingers just below your cheekbones and let your lips 'roll' to 'brrrr'. Practice going up and down a scale. Start low and gradually build up higher and higher!

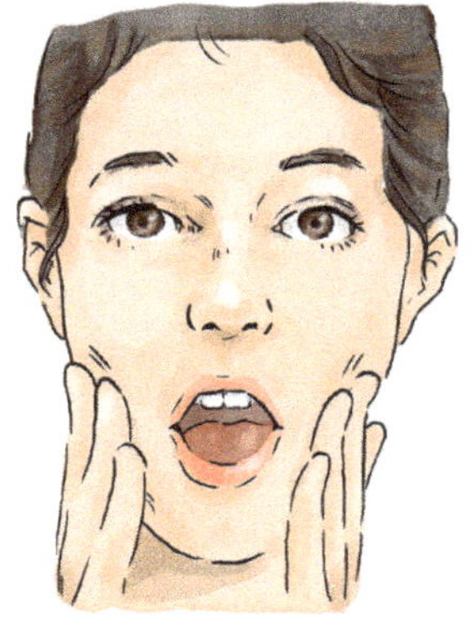

4. Straw Phonation:

Straw Phonation is when you utilise a straw to help you produce a sound. I first heard about Straw Phonation when I stumbled upon a video by Dr Ingo R. Titze. Straw Phonation has less impact and stress on the vocal folds, yet still stretching them in a balanced way.

Grab a small straw and blow through it. Try to keep the airflow consistent. Don't overcompensate the rate of air. Now, 'sing' through the straw the C Major scale. Gently blow the notes out. Well done! This time, I want you to 'sing' 'Twinkle, Twinkle Little Star' through the straw. No tension huh! I love this exercise!

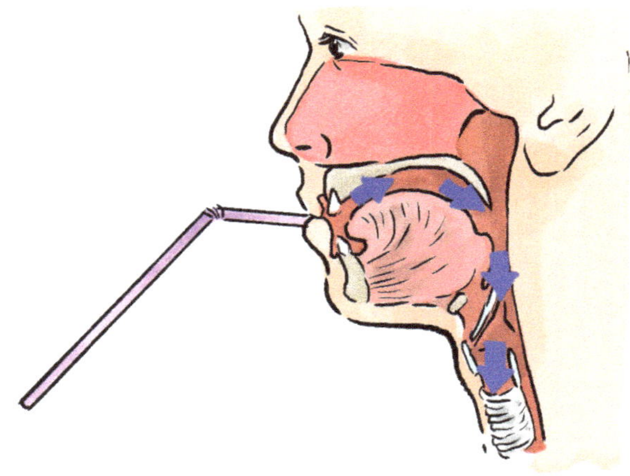

5. Squat & Sing

I incorporated this vocal exercise as I realized many of my students and clients wouldn't have the stamina to really move and sing at the same time. This not only makes sure you're keeping physically healthy, but also ensures that no matter how physically tired you may be, you can still sing and create a beautiful sound! It's all about control!

So what I want you to do is squat for me. You can do it! Whilst you squat, I want you to sing this exercise. Make sure your knees are bent, booty out a little, chest and shoulders relaxed, look forward and keep a neutral spine! Ready? Let's go!

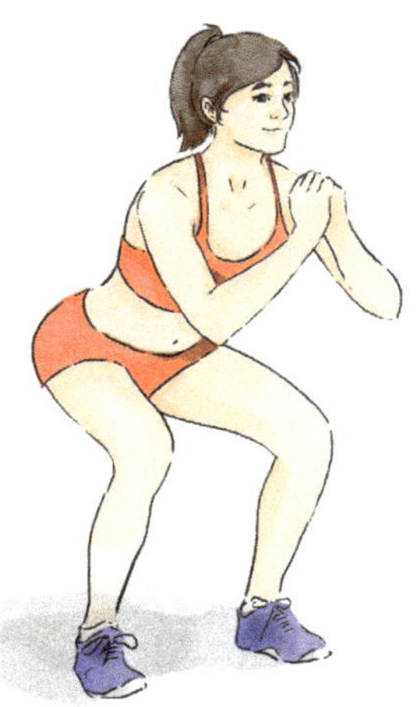

Squat & Sing Exercise

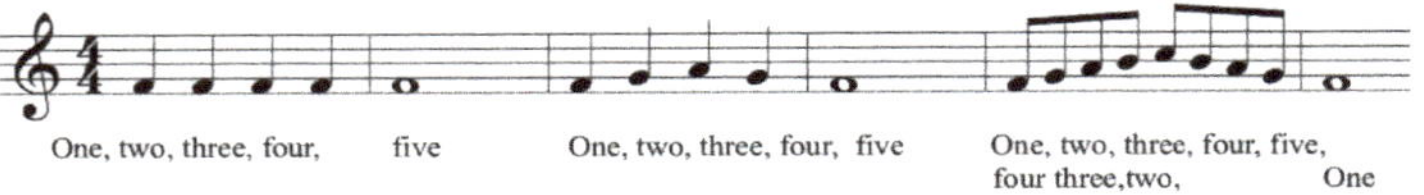

CHAPTER SIX

Vocal Harmonizing

Many people often ask me, 'Aarksara, how do I harmonize? How do I find the harmony? What if I can't hear the harmony? What if I'm out? In this chapter, I will break down simple harmonies with you. It's not as scary as you think they are! Don't over complicate it. First of all, let's find out what harmony is. Harmony is the combination of simultaneous musical notes in a chord that create a beautiful and pleasing sound. Harmonies enhance the sound of the song. You can have two-part, three-part, four-part, five-part and so forth harmonies. We will look at creating two-part harmonies in this course. There are four main voices: Soprano, Alto, Tenor and Bass (SATB) . Soprano is the highest female voice type. Altos are in the middle range. Tenors are the highest male voice types. Bass singers are the lowest male voice types. They sing the lowest notes.

Let's use the C Major scale to help us find harmonies. Harmonies are basically intervals to the 'home note'. Let's take 'C' as our home note.

Vocal Harmonizing Exercise

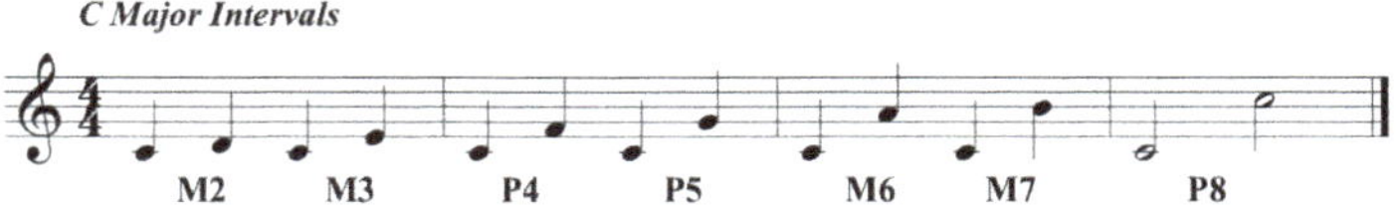

M2: Major 2nd
M3: Major 3rd
P4: Perfect 4th
P5: Perfect 5th
M6: Major 6th
M7: Major 7th
P8: Perfect 8th (Octave)

I want you to either download a 'Keyboard application' on your phone or use a real keyboard/piano to assist you with the exercise. First sing 'Oh' on the note C4. From there sing 'Oh' for the following intervals C4 to D4, C4 to E4, C4 to F4, C4 to G4, C4 to A4, C4 to B4, C4 to C5. Can you hear the smooth changes in the note intervals?

After you've done this exercise a few times, play the note C4 and pick an interval to sing without the assistance of a keyboard. Play the interval and see if you've sung the correct note! Harmony work is all about training the ear to hear the 'harmony line' that sits either above or below the melody line. Ultimately, all parts must **BLEND!**

Now, I want you to find a singing partner and practice the above exercise together! This time instead of singing 'Oh', sing 'Twinkle Twinkle Little Star' in the key of C. One person does the melody, the other person sings the harmony line- start with either singing the third or fifth interval line. Take turns singing the harmony lines!

Vocal Harmonizing Exercise II

CHAPTER SEVEN

Vocal Styling

Every music genre has its own set of vocal styling tools. Just like how we would style our clothes to a certain inspiration look, we would style our vocals according to our chosen music genre or vocal style. The main styles/genres of music include pop, rock, classical, country, blues/jazz and hip hop. Each musical style has its own special characteristics that make it unique.

Here is a list of different styles of music that exist in our world today:

Styles of Music

- A cappella
- Acid breaks
- Acid house
- Acid jazz
- Acid rock
- Acid techno
- Acid trance
- Acoustic
- Adult contemporary
- Afrobeat
- Afro-Cuban jazz
- Afropop
- Aguinaldo
- Aleatoric
- Alternative country
- Alternative dance
- Alternative hip hop
- Alternative metal
- Alternative R&B
- Alternative rock
- Ambient
- Ambient house
- Americana
- Anarcho-punk
- Anasheed
- Ancient
- Anatolian rock
- Anime
- Anti-folk
- Apala
- Arabic pop
- Argentine rock
- Ars antiqua
- Ars nova
- Ars subtilior
- Art pop
- Art punk
- Art rock
- Artcore
- Ashik
- Assyrian pop music
- Australian country
- Australian pub rock
- Australian hip hop
- Avant-garde
- Avant-garde jazz
- Avant-garde metal
- Avant-punk
- Axe
- Bachata
- Baggy
- Baguala
- Baiao
- Bakersfield sound
- Baila
- Baisha xiyue
- Bajourou
- Bal-musette
- Balakadri
- Balinese Gamelan
- Balearic beat
- Balkan Brass Band
- Ballad
- Ballata
- Ballet
- Baltimore Club
- Bambuco
- Banda
- Bagsawan
- Bantowbol
- Barbershop
- Barcarolle
- Barn dance
- Baroque
- Baroque pop
- Barynya
- Bass
- Bassline
- Bata-rumba
- Batucada
- Paul
- Beach
- Beat
- Beatboxing
- Beautiful
- Bebop
- Beguine/Biguine
- Beiguan
- Bel canto
- Bend-skin
- Benga
- Bent edge
- Bereju
- Berlin School
- Bhajan
- Bhangra
- Bhangragga
- Bio band
- Big beat
- Biguine
- Blackened death metal
- Black metal
- Black MIDI
- Bluegrass
- Blue-eyed soul
- Blues
- Blues ballad
- Blues rock
- Biomusic
- Bitpop
- Bihu
- Boogaloo
- Boenke-Boenke
- Boi
- Bossa Nova
- Bounce
- Bouncy techno
- Brass
- Breakbeat
- Breakbeat hardcore
- Breakcore
- Breakstep
- Brega
- Breton
- Brill Building Sound
- Brit Funk
- Britpop
- British blues
- British folk rock
- British Invasion
- Broken beat
- Brostep
- Brown-eyed soul
- Brukdown
- Bubblegum dance
- Bubblegum pop
- Bullerengue
- Bikutsi
- Bulerias
- Bunraku
- Burger-highlife
- Burgundian School
- Bush ballad
- Byzantine
- Ca din tulnic
- Ca tru
- Cabaret
- Cadence-lypso
- Cadence rampa
- Cai lu o ng
- Cajun
- Cakewalk
- Calinda
- Calgija
- Calypso
- Calypso-style balla
- Campursari
- Can Can
- Candombe
- Canon
- Cantata
- Cante Chico
- Cante jondo
- Canterbury scene
- Cantinas
- Cantiga
- Canto livre
- Cantopop
- Canzone Napoletana
- Capoeira
- Carimbo
- Cariso
- Carnatic
- Carol
- Cartageneras
- Carnavalito
- Cavacha
- Celempungan
- Cello rock
- Celtic
- Celtic fusion
- Celtic hip hop
- Celtic metal
- Celtic punk
- Celtic reggae
- Celtic rock
- Cha-cha-cha
- Chacarera
- Chakacha
- Chalga
- Chamame
- Chamarrita
- Chamber
- Chamber pop
- Champeta
- Changui
- Chanson
- Chant
- Chap hop
- Charanga-vallenata
- Charikawi
- Charleston (dance)
- Chastushka
- Chau van
- Cheo
- Children's music
- Chicago blues
- Chicago house
- Chicago soul
- Chicken scratch
- Chill-out
- Chillwave
- Chinese music
- Chinese rock
- Chiptune
- Chouval bwa
- Chowtal
- Choro
- Christmas carol
- Christmas music
- Christian electronic
- Christian alternative rock
- Christian country
- Christian hardcore
- Christian hip hop
- Christian metal
- Christian music
- Christian punk
- Christian rock
- Christian ska
- Chylandyk
- Chula
- Chumba
- Church music
- Chut-kai-pang
- Chutney
- Chutney Soca
- Cifra
- Cielito
- Classic country
- Classic female blues
- Classical
- Classical period
- Close harmony
- Coladeira
- Coldwave
- Combined ryhthm
- Comedy music
- Comedy rap
- Comedy rock
- Comic opera
- Compas
- Concerto
- Concerto grosso
- Conga
- Conjunto
- Contemporary Christian music
- Contemporary R&B
- Contradanza

Table Credit: Charlin Neal

If you take the Gospel Vocal Style as an example, a lot of vocal runs and riffs are used in this style.
The vocalist who would like to adapt this particular style can therefore practice his or her runs and riffs with exercises like singing connected notes slowly then gradually speeding up to create a seamless and smooth vocal riff/run.

Here are 5 vocal styles I would like you to research on. Write down at least 5 characteristics and particular vocal tools that are used to create this specific vocal style.

1. Musical Theatre:

____

____

____

2. Rock:

____

____

____

3. Pop:

____

____

____

4. Country:

____

____

____

5. Gospel:

____

____

____

CHAPTER EIGHT

SING!
Talk with my Soul Singing Sisters

Charlin Neal:

Worship Leader, Vocal Producer, Vocal Clinician, Vocal Arranger, Vocal Coach. Vocal Director for Israel Houghton and New Breed. I live to serve. I love God and my family!

Lois DuPlessis:

South African Actor, Singer and Worship Leader. Lois loves to see others win! She has a heart for serving and is walking out her path towards her destiny. She has had the privilege of sharing the stage with many phenomenal artists and feels blessed by the opportunities to share her story and experiences to help others grow. Lois has a passion for artist development and hopes to further pursue that in future.

Michelle Rossi:

Worship Leader. Backing Vocalist with Planetshakers, Vocal Coach at Planetshakers Creative School. I am passionate about living for Jesus and using my gifts and talents to honour Him.

What are your top 3 tips for singers?

Charlin : Have confidence in your voice. When you have confidence you can execute singing properly to avoid injuries and sounding very nicely. Take care of your voice. Your vocal chords are muscles, so sometimes they need a break. You only get one voice. Use it wisely. There's always room for growth. Expand your music library, to enhance your various stylings.

Michelle : It is important to practice, to make sure

you are well prepared before you ever perform and always be open to learning and developing your voice.

Lois : Know your voice, love your voice, and work with what you have, capitalizing on the strengths and continually working on the weaknesses!

Do you have any vocal routines before a performance?

Charlin : I try to make sure to have enough rest prior to any vocal performance. This doesn't always happen due to flights, family, etc. So when I am pressed for time, I limit my talking to refrain from talking too loud or yelling.

Michelle : I like to warm up my voice by doing a tongue stretch and stretch my body so that I'm relaxed and flexible. Then I do bubble trills following on a 5-tone and octave scale. Next I do Sirens on an 'oo' and 'ng' sound then hum on a 5-tone scale.

Lois : Pray, get quiet and focus, do vocal warm-ups and I often get on some music and dance.

Are there any particular foods/drinks you take before a performance?

Charlin : I drink lots of lukewarm water. I avoid drinking cold water two hours before, and two hours after singing. Every voice is different; this technique works for me. I also drink a tea called throat coat, and I place a cough suppressant called 'Ricola' in the tea.

Michelle : I like to drink plenty of water .I also

drink a throat coat tea and suck on propolis throat lozenges. If my voice is feeling a bit sore or tender I use the singer's' saving grace: throat spray. At the end of a show I will suck on ice.

Lois : I enjoy drinking hot water with honey and lemon before any meal. Before I sing I try not to eat but sometimes you can't stop that from happening depending on the setting you are in. I also use a tea called throat coat. I also use 'Ricola' lozenges when my voice is a bit tired. Food? I think it depends on the individual, what works for some does not always work for everyone when it comes to singing.

Who has been your favourite vocalist to work with in the studio and why?

Charlin : Daniel Johnson has been my favourite vocalist to work with in the studio. He's an incredible Vocal Producer who challenges me to do notes and sounds with my voice that sometimes I did not think I could do.

Michelle : That's a tough one I have a few peoplet hat I have worked with. Matt Gullaci, Karlee Brown and Scott Anderson to name a few.

Lois : Daniel Johnson. Not only did he encourage me to believe in the voice I have, he challenged me and taught me how to work with it! Under his direction I grew as a singer and for that I'm grateful!

Do you have any advice for singers who get nervous

before a performance?

Charlin : As a believer, I pray about everything. So when I am nervous, I pray. It calms my nerves and helps me to focus. Just relax, have confidence in yourself, in your voice, and just go for it.

Michelle : Take a deep breath. Tell yourself you can do this, because you have done all the practice and hard work. And be positive about yourself. I also like to pray before any performance.

Lois : Use the nervous energy to fuel your performance. Nerves are a good thing if you direct that energy to work for you! It becomes bad when you allow the nerves to overtake you, this will change your voice, affect your confidence and destroy your performance.

How do you handle mistakes during a performance?

Charlin : Recognise that I am not perfect, no one is. So with mistakes, I do not show it on stage. Chances are, half of the audience won't know you made a mistake. Behind closed doors, I fix my mistakes by practicing whatever part I messed up, that way I will be prepared for the next performance. Never show your mistakes in your face or body language!

Michelle : By smiling and just continuing on with the show. You can't change what happened but you can continue to still give your best for the rest of the show.

Lois : I always say "mess up confidently", most of the time the audience has no idea that you have messed up (except if you're singing in a room full of singers) so mess up but move on as if you have written that tiny mistake into your performance. Mess up and move on, you can't dwell on what has already happened. Accept it, work on improving yourself for the next time.

What inspires you as a vocalist?

Charlin : I am a music lover! Music inspires me. Different chords, sounds, beats inspire me to sing differently and write lyrics that I feel would enhance the music. Going through trials and down seasons in my life inspire me as well to sing out my frustrations, fears, desires and joys.

Michelle : People who are original and have a natural and raw talent. I appreciate and value those who stay true to who they are.

Lois : I'm a lyrics girl. If a song grabs me, 90% of the time it will be because of the lyrics. Different people have different styles, tones and delivery but the lyrics inspire me more than anything else. Writers like India Arie, Natasha Bedingfield and many more singer songwriters inspire me too!

CHAPTER NINE

Apps Every Vocalist Should Have

Metronome : https://itunes.apple.com/us/app/metronome-/id416443133?mt=8 I love this app! It is crucial for singers to learn how to sing in time! Start by singing ABC to 68BPM then gradually increase the speed to 72BPM, 76BPM, 80BPM etc.

Sing Friend : https://itunes.apple.com/us/app/singing-vocal-warm-ups-singers-friend/id350913803?mt=8 This is a great app to use for your vocal warm-ups on the go! It accommodates every voice range

Pocket Pitch : https://itunes.apple.com/th/app/pock-et-pitch- the-singer-app/id1005725401?mt=8: This is a great app for Pitch reference.

Perfect Piano : https://itunes.apple.com/us/app/perfect-piano-midi-keyboard/id942937409?mt=8: It is important singers know how to play basic scales on a keyboard/piano!

Terminology

- **Air Function/Air Flow :** How fast or slow air is passing through our mouth.

- **Chest Voice :** This voice resonates predominantly in the chest. It creates a rich, deep and full timbre.

- **Crescendo :** A gradual increase in loudness in a piece of music.

- **Decrescendo :** A gradual decrease in loudness in a piece of music.

- **Diaphragm :** Our diaphragm supports our vocal cords by automatically expanding.

- **Diction :** As singers, we want to make sure we communicate the message or story of the song by enunciating our words through our voice.

- **Flat Notes :** If we don't have enough air coming through, the notes we sing tend to fall flat. Flat notes are notes that are sung and pitched below the intended note.

- **Harmony :** The combination of simultaneous musical notes in a chord that create a beautiful and pleasing sound. Harmonies enhance the sound of the song.

- **Head Voice :** This voice resonates predominantly in the head. It usually produces a softer and airier sound.

- **Mixed Voice :** This is a combination of head and chest voice.

- **Nodules :** Tiny callous-like bumps on vocal cords

- **Polyps :** Lesions that are formed after a blood vessel is broken, similar to a blister.

- **Sharp Notes :** If we have too much air coming through, the notes we sing tend to sound sharp. Sharp notes are notes that are sung and pitched above the intended note.

- **Straw Phonation :** Using straw to help you produce a sound.

- **Timbre/Tones :** The emotional description of your voice. Interchangeable terms.

- **Vocal Abuse :** Occurs after extensive singing or speaking.

- **Vocal Placement :** Requires singers to properly position
their larynx so that the best possible sound is produced with ease.

Acknowledgements

Firstly, I want to thank God for allowing me to grow and learn in the gifts and skills He has given me. I won't be doing what I'm doing without Him. I pray U SING! will be a great blessing to everyone who reads it. I would like to thank my amazing family for their unending support. I love each and every single one of you. I am also grateful to my beautiful friends for their continuous encouragement. I want to also acknowledge all the incredible vocal teaching legends and scientists who have helped shape my understanding and created concepts and courses that I have been able to learn and adapt from: Brett Manning, Seth Riggs & Dr. Ingo R.Titze- just to name a few! Thank You. And to YOU who picked up this book, Thank YOU, I pray you will be blessed and equipped furthermore as a Vocalist.

Good days, **SING!**
Not so good days, **SING!**
Never stop **SINGING!**

— Aarksara —

www.ingramcontent.com/pod-product-compliance
Ingram Content Group UK Ltd.
Pitfield, Milton Keynes, MK11 3LW, UK
UKHW062255290726
14090UKWH00017B/703

9 786164 555617